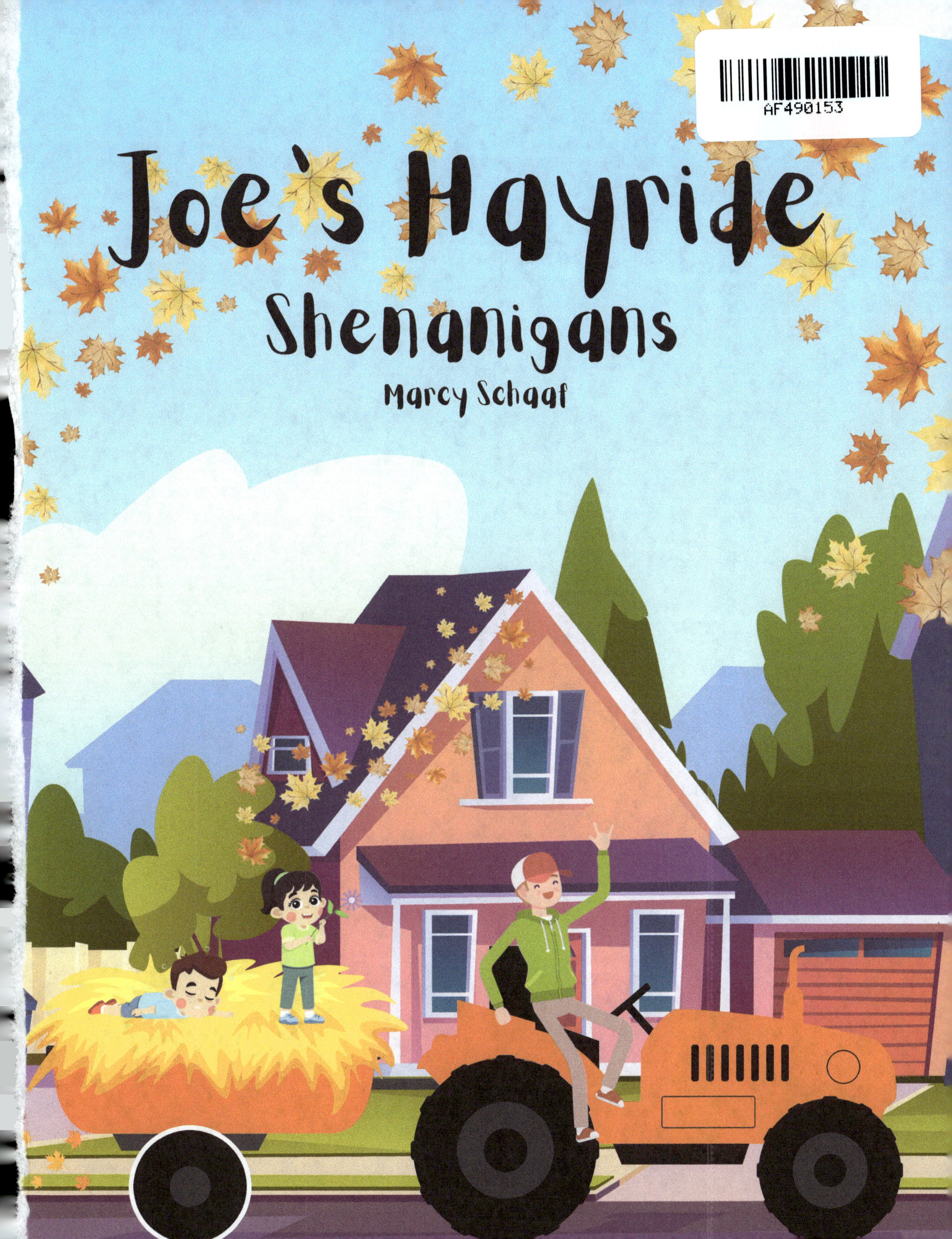

Joe's Hayride
Shenanigans
Marcy Schaaf
AF490153

Joe Schaaf had a great idea.

His wife was at work, and
the kids needed fun.

Joe looked at his
riding lawn mower.

He thought,
"I can make a hayride!"

Joe took the blades off carefully.

# He attached a wagon full of hay.

"Kids, come outside!"
Joe called loudly.

His kids ran out with
excitement in their eyes.

"Hop in! we're going for a ride!"

The neighborhood kids joined
the fun.

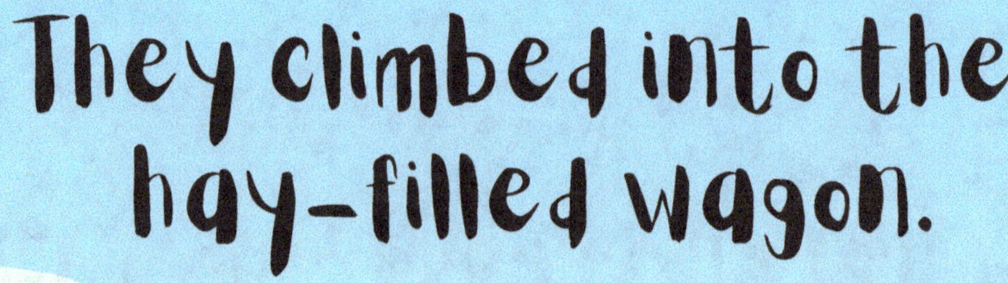

They climbed into the
hay-filled wagon.

And off they went.

They rode through the colorful
fall leaves.

Joe drove carefully, avoiding big bumps.

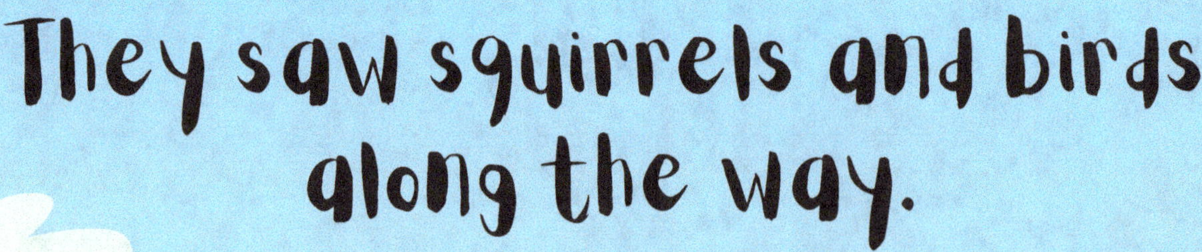

They saw squirrels and birds
along the way.

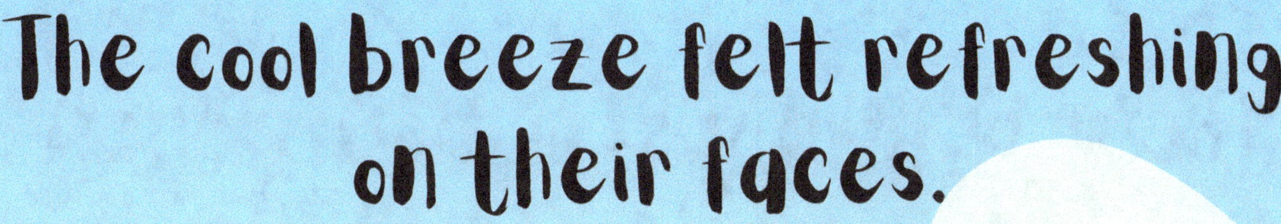

The cool breeze felt refreshing
on their faces.

Joe told funny stories as they rode.

# The kids loved Joe's entertaining tales.

# They made a stop at the big oak tree.